© Copyright 2015 — Regina McCollam
regina@imissionchurch.com

All rights reserved. This book is protected by the copyright laws of the United States of America. This book may not be copied or reprinted for commercial gain or profit. The use of short quotations or occasional page copying for personal or group study is permitted. Permission will be granted upon request. Scripture quotations are taken from the New American Standard Bible®, Copyright © 1960, 1962, 1963, 1968, 1971, 1972, 1973, 1975, 1977, 1995 by The Lockman Foundation. Used by permission. (www.Lockman.org)

Cover photo by Pali Rao © 2011
(iStock.com image 18796589)
Cover design by Regina McCollam

Interior photo by Esolla © 2013
(iStock.com image 23396575)

Author picture and photograph on page 25 by Dennis Watts

ISBN-13: 978-1508616405
ISBN-10: 150861640X

Printed in the United States of America.

Table of Contents

Introduction 1

The Wild Dance 3

Pensacola Road Dance 7

The Snake Dance 11

Fiji Line Dance 17

Wedding Dance 23

Conclusion 29

Introduction

*I*magine sitting alone at a sidewalk cafe watching life and its people going by. Close your eyes and really go there with me. What is the weather like? Is it a bright, cheery day? Is the sky grayed with a melancholy drizzle? Is it a quaint country town; or is it a bustling city street? Maybe it's a peaceful moment; life is fairly good. Maybe it's a difficult moment; life has plenty of challenges.

Whatever the circumstance, it doesn't really matter... what happens next is the same.

One so very strong yet kind, powerful yet self-controlled, commanding yet humble — one so perfect steps into your personal space nearly taking your breath away. He extends his hand to you and inquires, "May I have this dance?" Your heart races as you contemplate your response...

That's the invitation I feel from Heaven today. I hear Jesus asking each one of us, "May I have this dance?"

The chapters that follow are stories of times in my journey where I felt this invitation from Heaven, and a life transformation ensued. Coincidentally, each of these stories involves a literal dance. As you read, though, I hope you will understand that these stories are not just about me nor are their lessons limited to dance experiences. But the dance metaphorically represents Jesus' invitation to an upgrade in adventure and relationship with Him. As you read, I pray you will recall the times in your own journey when Jesus leaned in breathtakingly close to you and whispered, "May I have this dance?"

The Wild Dance—What Do You Mean?

*L*isten to the lyrics of this song that was potent in our worship services years ago:

> *I will not forget You are my God, my King*
> *And with a thankful heart*
> *I bring my offering*
> *And my sacrifice is not what You can give*
> *But what I alone can give to you*
>
> *A grateful heart I give,*
> *A thankful prayer I pray,*
> *A wild dance I dance before you*
> *A loud song I sing, A huge bell I ring,*
> *A life of praise I live before You*[1]

We were singing this song, and I was looking around the room. A few people were kicking their feet around in a bit of a dance, but *no one* was doing anything I would call a wild dance as the song was declaring. I certainly wasn't. I don't like to sing anything I don't mean, so I was asking, "What is the wild dance? Does it have anything to do with moving my feet to the music?

Listening to the song again..."what I alone can give to you...," I was asking, "But, God, every good and perfect thing comes from heaven above. What do we have that we have not been given? Is there anything I can give to You that You did not first give to me?"[2] It seemed to me the song was a farcical thing to be singing.

Of course, the answer was in the next verse of the song once I finally became aware of what I was actually singing. "A grateful heart... a thankful prayer... a life of praise I live before you..." I suddenly understood the life of praise I choose to live *is* the wild dance! A life truly lived in praise before God is a huge bell and a loud song that all can hear. It is a wild dance!

The dictionary definition of "wild" is "going beyond normal or conventional bounds" and also "indicative of strong passion, desire, or emotion."

I suddenly understood, also, that there is only one thing I, and I alone, can give to God. That one thing is *my choice* to give Him all of me. To live each day for Him and with Him. To choose Him in every decision. A grateful heart; a thankful prayer in every circumstance — *this is the wild dance* — and this is the one thing that only I can give to Him!

For to take His hand and let Him fully take the lead will take you on a wild path. It will be delightful. It will be fun. It will be frightening as He pulls you out of your comfort zones. It may feel confusing now and then. Not because He is the author of confusion,[3] but rather because His thoughts are higher than our thoughts.[4] It may even, at times, feel unfair or unjust as you lean into Him in obedience to a hard thing He is asking...only to eventually discover that even the hard things turn out for your own highest good, just as He promised.

One thing I know, choosing the wild dance will always be good, for He is good. So, when Jesus says to you, "May I have this dance?" your "yes" is the only thing that you alone can give to Him. Anyone can choose the slow dance — rocking back and forth, going with the flow—but your life of uncompromising praise, thanks, and obedience is the wild dance you, and only you, can choose to dance before Him.

The Pensacola Road Dance — Second Chances

Then there is the dance of second chance.

One of the first times I remember Jesus extending His hand to me in an invitation to rise and dance happened almost 20 years ago.

I went on a trip to Pensacola, Florida, to visit what was called the Brownsville Revival (aka the Pensacola Outpouring). I road on a bus 17 hours with folks I had never met before. I slept in a hotel bed with a stranger, and stood in line for hours with hundreds of others hoping to get a seat in the packed auditorium at the

Brownsville Assembly of God church. All of this outside of my usual comfort zone.

All heaven was breaking loose in the Brownsville Revival meetings held four nights a week for five straight years, and a seat to witness it was worth gold. When I finally reached the entrance to the auditorium, barely daring to hope there would be any room left, an usher looked at me and said, "Are you by yourself?"

"Yes," I replied.

"I have just the seat for you," he declared as he took my arm and marched me up to the second row right in front of the piano being played by the now famous worship leader, Lindell Cooley. The service itself was a great experience where Holy Spirit was talking to me about *us* the whole time—but that is another story. My story now is about the bus ride home.

A couple of hours into the 17-hour drive home, there was a video recording of one of the revival services playing on the bus TV system. Lindell was enthusiastically leading the song, "I Went to the Enemy's Camp (and I took back what he stole from me)."[5] It was a lively chorus that begged to be danced to. In my spirit, I heard Jesus invite me to get up and dance.

"What?! Right here? Right now? On the bus? Where? In the middle of this skinny aisle? No!"

The irrepressible invitation kept pulling at me as the song continued on, every second getting closer to its inevitable conclusion and the end of my opportunity to obey. I just couldn't do it. No. So, the song ended; the music stopped. Regret immediately came rushing in. "I'm so sorry, God! I'm so sorry. I'll do it. I will. If they play that song again, I will dance," I offered.

Think about it—what are the chances of the song playing again? This is a prerecorded video playing across the bus-wide TV system late in the night while driving along some interstate highway in Alabama.

Well, as though that whole previously recorded worship service had happened just for me and the future personal invitation I would receive from my Prince to dance with Him on that bus that very night, Lindell kicked up that song again! As he belted out, "I went to the enemy's camp, and I took back what he stole from me, took back what he stole from me, took back what he stole from me...," I jumped out of my seat and did my ridiculous jig right there in that narrow bus aisle, to the sleepy surprise of my fellow passengers as we bumped along the highway. I felt so stupid yet ever so grateful for God's patience and inevitable invitation to a second chance.

Did anything grand happen right then and there? Well, no...not that I could see anyway. But I believe that every time we respond to Jesus' invitation to step out with Him, the band strikes up in the heavens. Who knows but that one response to dance with the Prince didn't open up the way for the day, some years later, that I truly did dance right into the devil's camp and indeed took back what he stole from me.

The Snake Dance—You Make Me Brave

I grew up a very shy person, the third child in a family of six siblings. Finding a place to hide and stay out of the way was normal for me. Near perfect obedience was easier than taking any risk to venture into the unknown world of curious teenagers, so I was perceived as an angel child—such a good girl. I have since understood that my "good girl" lifestyle had little to do with holiness and more to do with taking the easy way out like most everybody else. For me, the easier route was to stay inside the boundaries.

So, I grew into a very shy woman. My heart and my spirit longed for adventure, but fearful is who I was. Shy was who God made me to be, and I could live with that. I learned to carry myself tall and even fully enjoy the life of safety I led inside my bubble of intimidation.

I could live without the friendships that fear kept me from pursuing. I could live without the freedom to love and minister to others. I could live without allowing my personal dreams to grow in my spirit—as that would take me out of my comfort zone. I could accept the fact that I just wasn't going to be what I saw in others that I longed for so much. I truly knew that Jesus loved me just the way I was, and I loved Him too. That was truth, and it seemed to be a happy life.

But then one day, my Savior stood up. He extended His hand to me and asked, "May I have this dance?"

It was another conference, seemingly not unlike any other of the endless conferences I had attended as a minister's wife. There I sat on the front row, only because I was the minister's wife. I'd much rather have been safely in a cocoon further back in the auditorium seating.

Michal Ann Goll was on stage speaking into the microphone a word of encouragement before the main speaker came forward with that night's intended message. She was speaking about the Old Testament woman Jael (ya-el) who killed Israel's enemy when he fled from the army right to her tent door. Jael had invited the enemy king into her home where he eventually made himself comfortable enough to take a nap. While that king was sleeping, Jael drove a tent peg through his temple, killing him and winning the battle for all of Israel. Victory came at the hands of a woman, just as the prophet had predicted.[6]

Michal Ann was asking, "What if God brought your enemy right to your doorstep?" In her message, she specifically mentioned the enemy of fear and intimidation. The woman sitting next to me dug her elbow into my side and declared, "Oh, you deal with that all the time, don't you?"

"What?!" I was horrified! I was well aware of the fearful place I lived, but I didn't know it was written all over me. I didn't know how obvious my bondage was to those around me. In fact, I didn't even know it was a bondage. But in that moment, Jesus lifted the veil from my eyes, and I saw the enemy of my life for what it really was. In a matter of seconds, maybe minutes, Jesus told me that shy was not a personality trait He had designed for me but rather a lie the enemy used to control me. Jesus showed me how I had been robbed all my life and offered me an invitation of choice — "May I have this dance?" He was asking.

I began to see in my spirit a movie playing back all the missed opportunities that fear and intimidation had robbed me of. As scene after scene from my entire life flashed before my spiritual eyes, I became more and more filled with what I can only describe as holy rage. "I've been robbed!" my spirit screamed, "My whole life long I HAVE BEEN ROBBED!"

It was at this point that I again became aware of Michal Ann on the conference stage just as she said, "Well, why don't you just go ahead and kill that snake!" That was all the invitation I needed for my boiling spirit to burst forth..., "Yes, Jesus, let's have this dance!"

I jumped out of that front row seat and began to stomp and spin and scream. I could literally feel the snake of fear and intimidation under my feet, and I danced and stomped until I felt it die! Once the deed was done, I stopped spinning, shook my finger at that dead snake and hissed, "I dare you to stick your ugly head up again!" Then I straightened my tousled hair and dress and sat back down.

Realizing at that point that none of the other 2,000 people in that auditorium had made such a scene, I thought I had better explain. So I stood back up and declared, "I killed that snake!"

When I woke the next morning, I knew I was different. I knew that the fearful, intimidated place I had lived all my life was gone, and I was never going back! I could only exclaim, "This is what freedom feels like? This is what you people have felt all along?" Dear God, I didn't even know I was in bondage! I have gone only forward since that day—baby steps some days; giant leaps on others; but grateful every single day.

Thank you, Jesus, for patiently and lovingly waiting for Your opportunity to invite me into the dance over our enemy. Thank you for venturing past the walls of my fear and asking at just the right moment for the dance of a lifetime. Thank you for giving me the courage to say yes. You make me brave.

Fiji Line Dance—
Save the Next Dance for Me

     *L*ine dancing...everyone doing the same steps, making the same moves. Oh, sure, everyone has their own style. Some move freely and with pizzazz; some stiffly try to keep step. Ah, so much easier for me than freestyling! At least someone is guiding me with which move to make next. One thing I have learned, line dancing is so much more comfortable in a crowd where you can blend in a little.

    I was in Fiji on a missions trip with a group from our church. The first service we held there was an all-day women's gathering. Deb (our pastor's wife) spoke to the ladies about how it is possible to really know God, to be close to Him and He to you, to be intimate with Him and see Him face to face. She told us that to know God, at times, means to wrestle with Him as Jacob did in Genesis 32. In these wrestlings, we are changed; God marks our lives, and we never walk the same again.

Halfway through that great day, 20 or so Fijian women lined up across the front of the room in two lines. Music started up, and they danced for us one of the traditional Fijian line-type dances. The motions of their hands and feet were telling the story of the song—kind of like a Hawaiian hula dance, though not nearly as graceful. As they went through the motions over and over again, I found myself wanting to jump up and join them! Do I dare? Would it be proper? God, is that You asking me to dance?

By the time I took so long figuring out if it was God urging me or not, the song ended. Opportunity missed. Suddenly I was horrified that perhaps it really was God, and I had disobeyed. "I'm sorry, God. I'm trying to hear Your voice. Why do I always second-guess what I think is You?"

It's because of fear—oh, there's that ugly word again! Fear of making a mistake, fear of failure, fear of punishment. Yet, there is no fear in love...so I've heard. Perfect love casts out fear, because fear involves punishment, 1 John 4:18 tells us.

> *There is no fear in love; but perfect love casts out fear, because fear involves punishment, and the one who fears is not perfected in love.*

What is this punishment that we are all so afraid of? That God will be disappointed that we stepped out in faith—doesn't it sound ridiculous when spoken aloud? God's love does not involve punishment. Therefore, there is no punishment when we step out in God. Even when we make a mistake, He turns it to good. Even when we fall, He raises us up to an even higher place. You can't possibly go wrong when you are living under this love. Yet the one who fears, 1 John 4:18 continues, is not perfected in this love. In other words, the one who allows fear to interfere, reveals that she has not fully come to know and believe the love God has for her—the perfecting love that would shape and complete her if it were allowed to have its way.[7]

Guess what? In that Fijian pavilion, the song started over again as another group got up to do a different version of the same dance—only this time there were just four of them. Well, I got the message. It would have been a lot easier to obey the first time with more people to blend in with, but here I go! I watched just long enough to get familiar with the motions and then asked permission from the Fijian leader to join them. I said, "Would they like it if I danced with them?" She fervently shook her head up and down. Wondering if she really understood my English, I asked again, "Would they be happy if I danced with them?"

"Yes. Yes," she responded. Well, okay then! I ran up and joined the dance. I dared not even look up lest I fall apart from embarrassment. Keeping my eyes glued to the dear Fijian dancer next to me—who, by the way, was quite surprised to see me there—I finished the entire dance with them.

Since having this revelation of the ability of God's perfect love to cast out fear, I have been putting it to the test by stepping into some things I would have shied away from before. I have been venturing to believe that I am who God says I am and taking some risks that go along with that belief.

It hasn't all been glamorous. I've made some ignorant and painful mistakes and some relational messes that I've had to clean up along the way. One time my elementary-aged son got into enough trouble at school that the teacher gave me a call. As I was apologizing profusely for my usually well-behaved child's mischief, the teacher interrupted me. "Oh, no," she said, "I am so proud of your son. The students who never take a risk are the ones who never get into trouble. I am not complaining about him; I am reporting to you his bravery!" I actually heard God tell me once, "I think your mistakes are adorable."

So, yes, I've made some clumsy mistakes as I've responded to God's invitation to a higher call, but, even so, I always feel the pleasure of my dance partner as He pulls me in close with those stalwart arms and whispers in my ear, "Thank you for letting Me take the lead. Thank you for stepping out."

Wedding Dance — Comparison is a Rip-Off

I hate public dances. In fact, I'm not sure I even believe in them as a place a believer needs to spend time. No condemnation intended—it's just my personal opinion. Yet, here I was, at a public dance at my own son's wedding cringing as I heard the DJ shout over the public address system, "Let's get this party started!" The driving beat blared as the young people, joined by a scattering of brave middle-aged guests, bopped up and down and side to side to the rhythm. Staring into the gyrating group, I was thinking, "You know, that actually looks like fun. If I knew anything about dancing, I just might join them."

As my daydream continued, my attention was caught by my alarmingly beautiful eight-year-old, junior-bridesmaid daughter sitting alone staring into the dancing crowd with the same longing look I was wearing. She was so lovely this day with her deep purple gown and long blonde hair swept into a princess braid adorned with sparkling rhinestone clips. She even wore Mama's dangly jeweled earrings, a privilege she is normally not allowed. Yet, her especially captivating look is not what caught my attention just then, but the sad expression of longing she was wearing on her face. "Oh, no," I thought, "I recognize that look." Way too often I've experienced that wishing I was brave enough to join the group having so much fun doing the things I felt I could never do. I spent most of my life in that regretful place; I cannot watch my daughter live her lifetime under the same weight. This cannot happen.

Just then she walked over to me and confessed, "I don't know how to dance."

"Neither do I," I responded.

Regina and Tambre 2015

We sat together and watched the laughing dancers for a minute or two. I was thinking about how comparing ourselves to others is such a rip-off.

"Look at them," I instructed. "None of them know how to dance! They are just wiggling to the music each one in their own way. Not one of them is wiggling better than another." Realizing that if my words were going to hold any weight, I was going to have to prove it. I was going to have to overcome my own fear of comparison and incompetence and get out on that dance floor. I would have to lead the way!

Putting on my bravest face, I took my gorgeous, black lace, high-heeled wedding shoes out on that dance floor and joined the party. Oh, I felt so silly! It soon paid off, though, as my sweet little girl stepped tentatively onto the designated dance space. "Good girl!" I delightedly thought, "I don't care if you attempt a single dance move or wiggle those cute little hips one inch, I am so proud of you for taking the first step!"

Hey, nobody knows completely what they are doing in this dance we call "living by faith." We watch; we listen; we learn; and then we just do it. Perfection is not the goal, and baby steps are okay with God. Just get out there on that dance floor!

I may not be the most graceful, but I have come to understand that when Jesus asks me to dance, it is because He wants to dance with *me*. He is not comparing me with another; He is choosing *me*. And whatever the challenge that lay ahead, I can step forward with confidence knowing that Jesus chose *me* because He wanted *me*.

He knows who I am and who I am not. He knows what I can and cannot do. He even knows the part of who I am that I have yet to discover, and when He asks me to dance, I know He is inviting me into that discovery.

So I step into His powerful arms and let Him take the lead, and the wild dance commences.

Conclusion

We began this short journey of stories by comparing our passionate pursuit of a life in intimate relationship with Jesus Christ to a wild dance. My experiences have unraveled what I am sure are common robbers lurking along the highway of this passionate pursuit. Let's remember them one more time so we will never forget how powerless they are when submitted to the lover of our souls.

Indecision and delayed obedience bring introspection that causes even more hesitation and fear rather than the wild leap of faith our spirits are so willing for. "The spirit is willing, but the flesh is weak."[8] Hmmm, why do we always take that to mean the flesh is likely to win out? What part of "weak" is so hard to understand? Our spirits are ready and willing!

Another robber is **false identity of any kind** that says you can't, you don't know how, you are not good enough, you are disqualified—all of these lies can be trampled under the feet of a wild dance with Jesus. Our God of peace promises to crush Satan underneath our feet.[9] Let's wildly believe we are who He says we are, and we can be what He says we can be.

Fear in all its ugly forms is another stumbling block that we can choose to leap over. Eleanor Roosevelt said, "No one can make you feel inferior without your consent."[10] I know it's painful to admit, but I believe this is true. And I believe it applies to the devil's attempts to intimidate us as well!

My pastor in Kentucky[11] often asked us, "When was the last time you did something for the first time?" I love days like that—when I cross over a line of fear or attempt something new—they are downright exhilarating!

Oh, yeah, and don't forget that robber of **comparison**. It keeps us longingly gazing from the sidelines saying, "I don't know how to dance like that." We can count on our helper Holy Spirit to teach us the steps; our responsibility is only to bravely accept the invitation.

But I don't want to focus on these robbers any more. Let's go back to that sidewalk cafe where we first began this chat. I think the clouds have cleared, and a ray of sunshine is sparkling on the crystal table setting. The One has stepped into your personal space. I can almost hear your heart racing, and, even though He is leaning ever so close to your ear, I can hear Jesus whispering, "May I have this dance?" Your breath catches as you contemplate your answer...

Endnotes

[1] "I Will Not Forget," written by Ben and Robin Pasley. Copyright © 1999 Blue Renaissance Music (SESAC)

[2] See 1 Corinthians 4:7 and James 1:17.

[3] See 1 Corinthians 14:33.

[4] See Isaiah 55:9.

[5] "Enemy's Camp," words and music by Richard Black. Copyright ©1991 Sound III, Inc. ASCAP
You can see the song performed at a Brownsville Revival meeting at this YouTube link:
https://www.youtube.com/watch?v=7Jgye4hAhfM

[6] See Judges 4-5.

[7] See also 1 John 4:16.

[8] See Matthew 26:41.

[9] See Romans 16:20.

[10] *This is My Story,* by Eleanor Roosevelt, Garden City Publishing, inc., 1939.

[11] Cleddie Keith at Heritage Fellowship, 7216 US 42, Florence, KY 41042.

INTERTWINED
Strength to Stand
By Regina McCollam

This pictorial book parallels the living example of community displayed by the Coastal Redwood forest with what Romans 12 describes as "love without hypocrisy." Using photographic images and an original paraphrase of Romans 12:9-18, proclamations are made that line up with Christ's command to "love one another as I have loved you."

**Available at Amazon.com and
http://store.imissionchurch.com**

Printed in Poland
by Amazon Fulfillment
Poland Sp. z o.o., Wrocław